THE OFFICIAL WORKBOOK
MINECRAFT
KINDERGARTEN

Written by Russell Ginns

Illustrations by Antonio Vecchione

WELCOME TO A LEARNING ADVENTURE!

This workbook lets kids practice essential skills while taking a journey through the world of Minecraft. Learn to count while taming a wolf and learn about patterns by escaping a polar bear! There are dozens of activities filled with reading, math, and critical-thinking skills, all set among the biomes, mobs, and loot of your child's favorite game.

Special Minecraft Missions at the end of each lesson also send readers on learning challenges inside and outside the book!

Here are some tips to make the most of this workbook:

- Make sure your child has a quiet, comfortable place to work.

- Give your child a variety of pencils, crayons, and any other items they may need to write answers, draw pictures, or set up games.

- Read the directions with your child. There's a lot of information and adventures packed into each chapter! You can help tell the stories and point out the basic tasks that need to be done.

- Spend extra time on any section that your child finds difficult.

- Enjoy the fun Minecraft facts and jokes with your child. This is your chance to learn more about a game that interests them!

Grab a pen or pencil and get ready to have fun as you learn with Minecraft!

MINECRAFT EXPLORE

WELCOME TO MINECRAFT

You've arrived in an exciting new place. Start by gathering resources.

In this adventure, you will...

Punch trees.

Collect sticks and wood.

Craft planks.

Make a crafting table.

Let's get started!

You are wandering through the forest. Punch some trees to get your first resource—wood.

Trace, then write big **A**.

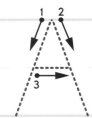

Trace, then write little **a**.

Draw a line from the player to all the trees with the letter **A** or **a**.

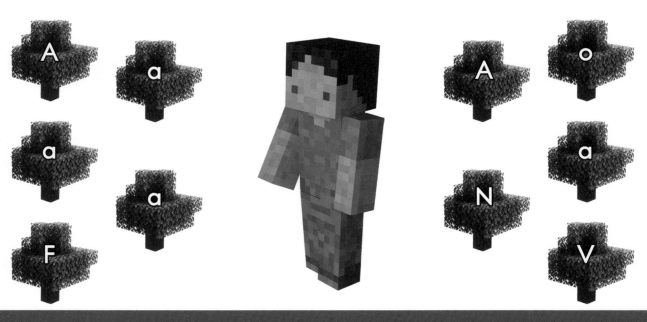

MINECRAFT FACT: Wood tools are usually the first set of tools that a player will craft in Minecraft.

Trace, then write big **B**.

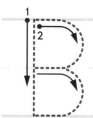

Trace, then write little **b**.

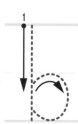

Circle all the wood with the letter **B** or **b**.

Collect as much wood as you can from the forest. You can use it to make so many helpful tools.

Trace, then write big C.

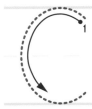

Trace, then write little c.

Trace, then write big D.

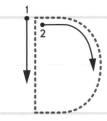

Trace, then write little d.

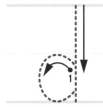

MINECRAFT FACT: Forests usually have only one type of wood in each area.

Find a path through this forest from **START** to **END**.
You can only pass through **C**, **c**, **D**, or **d**.

START

A
d
C
b

i
y

f
z
b
j
g
D
d
W
K
M

a
c
O

G

H

B
C

T
r
o
C

a
c

p
d
d
P

v
D

END

Craft planks with wood. They are good for making tools, structures, and many other useful things.

Trace, then write big **E**.

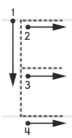

Trace, then write little **e**.

Write the letter **e** to complete the words.

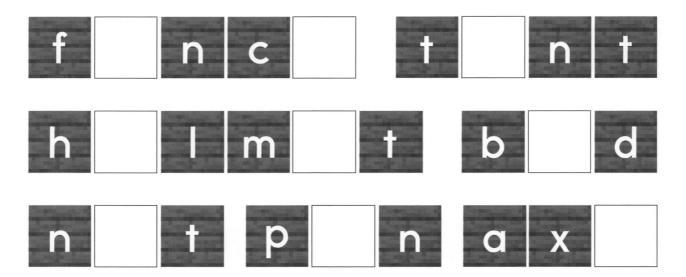

MINECRAFT FACT: Crafting two wood planks together makes four sticks.

Trace, then write big **F**.

Trace, then write little **f**.

Circle everything that has an **f** in its name. The first one has been done for you.

 bowl　　 (firecharge)　　 sunflower

 clownfish　　 flint　　 shovel

 boat　　 bow　　 fishing rod

 campfire　　 arrow　　 sword

How many **f**'s did you find? _____

You did it! Place your sticker here.

A crafting table will help you use your wood planks to make many things you'll need on your Minecraft adventure.

Trace, then write big **G**.

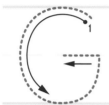

Trace, then write little **g**.

Draw lines to complete each word.

 e

 d

 ga

 ge

t

gg

og

p

What did the explorer say when someone gave them wood? *"Planks very much."*

Trace, then write big **H**.

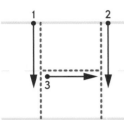

Trace, then write little **h**.

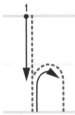

Circle every **H** or **h**.

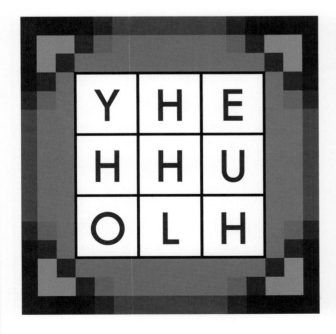

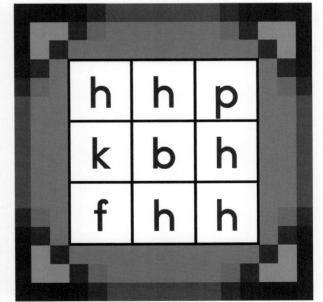

MINECRAFT MISSION

Now that you've learned a bit about the world of Minecraft, explore *your* world with a special challenge.

This mission sends you *outside* of this book! Your task is to explore the different regions of your house in search of items that fit these rules:

- Find **1** thing that starts with the letter **a**
- Find **2** things that start with the letter **b**
- Find **3** things that start with the letter **c**
- Find **3** things *inside*—one each starting with **d**, **e**, and **f**
- Find **2** things *outside*—one each starting with **g** and **h**

Cross out the letters as you find each thing.

| a | b | b | c | c | c | d | e | f | g | h |

When you are done, find the correct sticker and place it in the lower corner. You've completed your first mission!

MINECRAFT EXPLORE

Great job! You earned a badge! Place your sticker here.

DANGER!

Night is falling... and with it comes danger. Creepers are on the loose!

In this adventure, you will...

Outrun creepers.

Reach a clearing.

Avoid damage.

Survive the night.

Let's get started!

Outrun creepers and get out of reach!

Trace, then write the number 1.

Trace, then write the word **one**.

Circle all the groups that have **one** creeper.

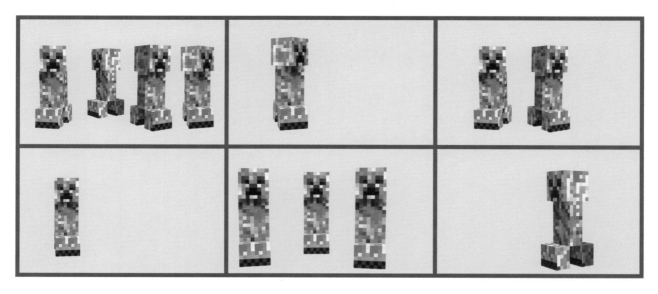

Trace, then write the number **2**.

Trace, then write the word **two**.

Draw a **square** (□) around **two creepers** (🟩).

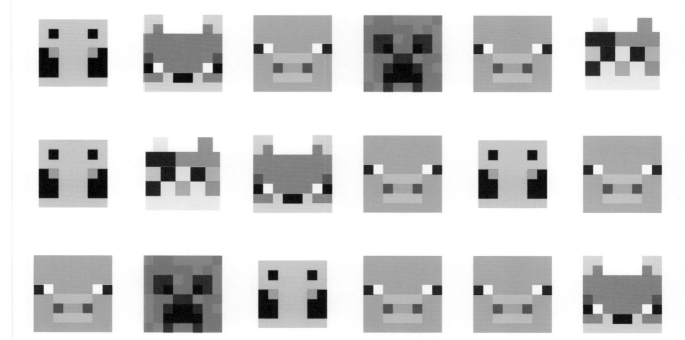

You've made it to an open area. Make sure you keep some distance from mobs.

Trace, then write the number **3**.

Trace, then write the word **three**.

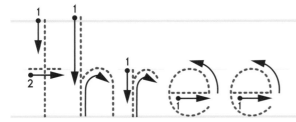

Cross out **three hostile mobs** (▨ ▨ ▨).

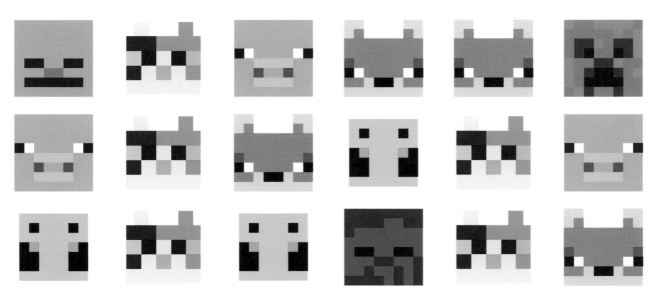

MINECRAFT FACT: Being in an open area makes it easier to keep an eye on mobs.

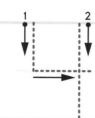
Trace, then write the number **4**.

Trace, then write the word **four**.

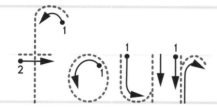

Draw a **square** (□) around the groups that have **four creepers** (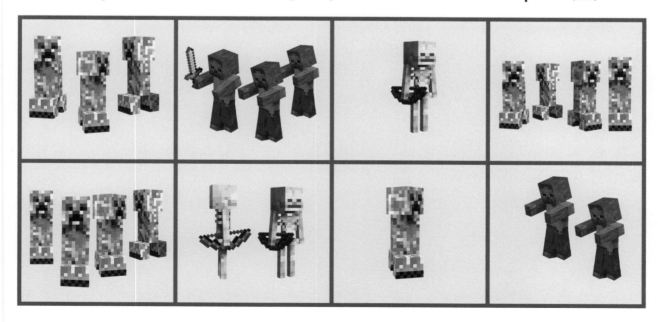).

If you hear a creeper hissing, it's about to explode! Stay alert to avoid damage.

Trace, then write the number **5**.

Trace, then write the word **five**.

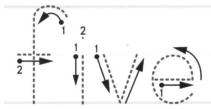

Trace, then write the number **6**.

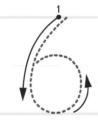

Trace, then write the word **six**.

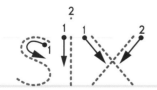

MINECRAFT FACT: Creepers may explode when they get within three blocks of you.

Trace, then write the number **7**.

Trace, then write the word **seven**.

Count and write the number of creepers in each row. Don't count the ones that are exploding.

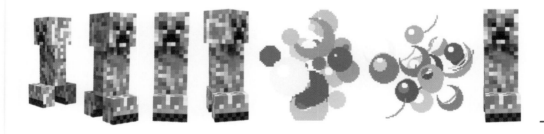

Wooden, stone, or gold swords are good for getting rid of creepers. Put your sword to use!

Trace, then write the number **8**.

Trace, then write the word **eight**.

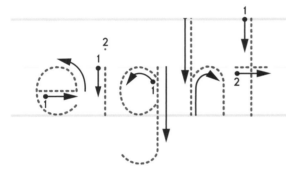

Trace, then write the number **9**.

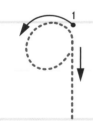

Trace, then write the word **nine**.

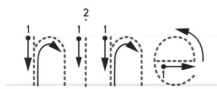

What happened to the creeper who lost the race? He came in blast place!

Trace, then write the number 10.

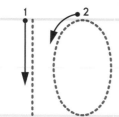

Trace, then write the word **ten**.

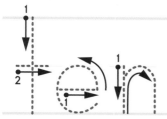

Cross out **eight gold swords** (✗). Then cross out **ten wood swords** (✗).

Count and write the number of swords that are left. _____

MINECRAFT MISSION

You've escaped from your enemies. Now go on a mission to search for other lurking foes.

This mission sends you on a search *inside* this book. There are items hidden in the top borders of most pages!

Write the page number where you find each one. The first one has been done for you.

22

Find the correct sticker and place it in the lower corner when you're done!

MINECRAFT SURVIVE

Great job! You earned a badge! Place your sticker here.

MINECRAFT
BUILD

A ROOF OVER YOUR HEAD

Make a nice place to stay and remain safe.

In this adventure, you will....

Clear an area.

Build walls.

Make floors and windows.

Greet visitors.

Let's get started!

Clear a flat area for a home.

Trace, then write big **I**.

Trace, then write little **i**.

Draw a line from the player to all the blocks with the letter **I** or **i**.

MINECRAFT FACT: Shovels help you dig dirt, sand, and gravel much faster than other tools.

Trace, then write big **J**.

Trace, then write little **j**.

Circle all the blocks that have a **J** or **j**.

J	r	j	J	j	E	J	f	m	t
B	x	j	J	j	J	j	V	b	z
U	I	J	j	J	h	J	J	S	j
A	J	J	j	Y	J	j	C	I	W
Q	j	G	J	j	N	D	j	B	J

Use buildings and walls to keep away mobs and protect you at night.

Trace, then write big **K**.

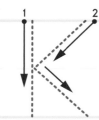

Trace, then write little **k**.

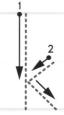

Trace, then write big **L**.

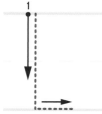

Trace, then write little **l**.

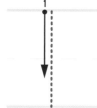

MINECRAFT FACT: Players are two blocks tall. Make your walls three blocks tall to enable you to jump inside your house.

Escape these mobs! You can only pass through **K**, **k**, **L**, or **I**.

Fix up your new place! Add a floor and lanterns for light!

Trace, then write big **M**.

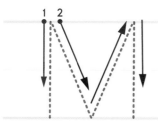

Trace, then write little **m**.

Write the letter **m** to complete each word.

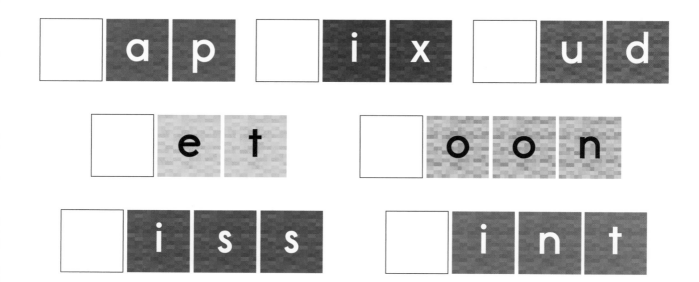

MINECRAFT FACT: You can make glass by smelting sand in a furnace.

Trace, then write big **N**.

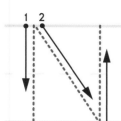

Trace, then write little **n**.

Circle everything that has an **n** in its name. The first one has been done for you.

(horn)   book   boat

 lantern   bone   candle

 shovel   plank   banner

How many **n**'s did you find? _____

You've got new neighbors! They're here to greet you.

Trace, then write big O.

Trace, then write little o.

Circle the villagers who are thinking of words that have o.

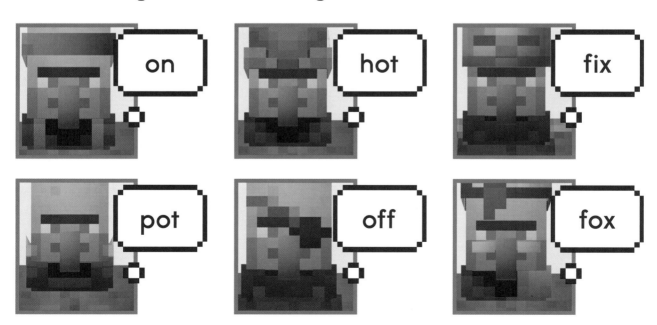

Why couldn't the mobs get through the walls?   They were blocked!

Trace, then write big **P**.

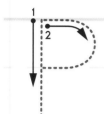

Trace, then write little **p**.

Cross out every villager that has **P** or **p**.

Write the letters you didn't cross out and read the word: _____

MINECRAFT MISSION

You're in your home, safe among your villager friends. Make your room in real life a special place to stay too.

This mission is a project *outside* of this book! Decorate your room with art that uses some of the words below.

You'll need:

- Crayons
- Paper
- Pencils
- Scissors
- Tape

Add one letter to complete each of the words below.

Then make signs to decorate your room. Use one word from the list on each sign!

__pen   welco__e

morn__ng   kee__

ro__m   he__lo

MINECRAFT BUILD

Great job! You earned a badge! Place your sticker here.

WHAT'S THE BUZZ?

Bee nests are good for harvesting honey and helping crops to grow.

In this adventure, you will....

Discover bees.

Avoid stings.

Lead the bees to flowers.

Pollinate.

Let's get started!

Look over there! It's a bee nest on a tree.

Help the adventurer find a path from **START** to the tree at **END**.

Read the numbers as you move from space to space. You must pass through the numbers I to **20** in order!

If you land on a **bee** ( )...whoops! Start over.

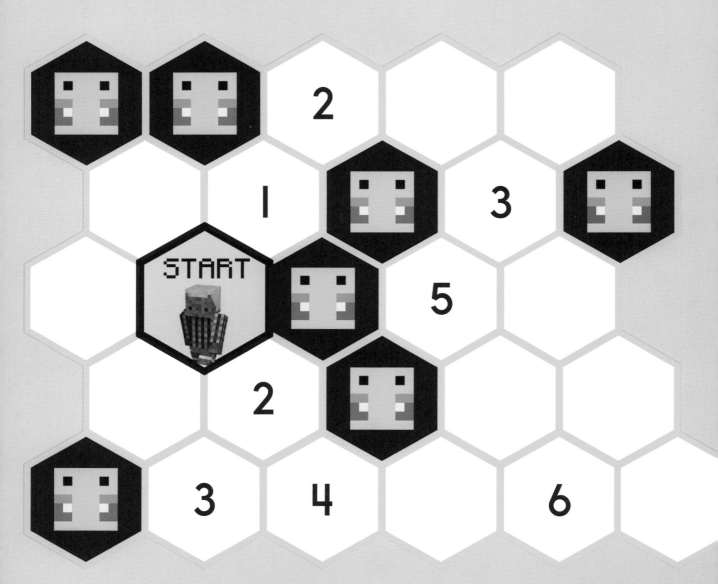

MINECRAFT FACT: If a player hits a bee, all nearby bees will become angry.

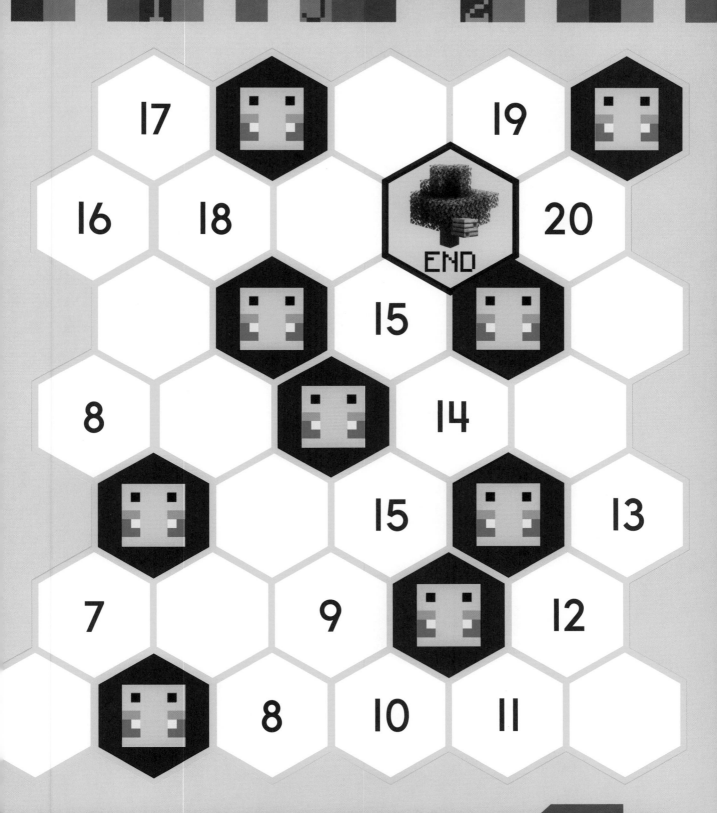

You did it! Place your sticker here.

Be careful around bee nests. You don't want to get stung!

Count the bees in each group and write the number.

_____

_____

_____

MINECRAFT FACT: Bees are slow. Sprint to stay away from their stings.

36

Circle **20** bees.

You did it! Place your sticker here.

Craft a beehive near flowers by your house.

Write the missing numbers.

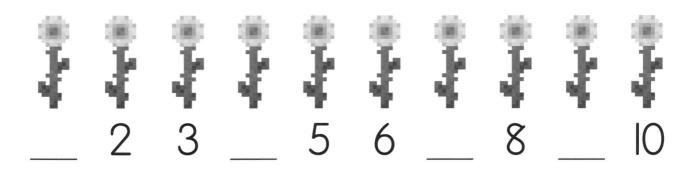

1 2 3 4 __ 6 7 __ 9 10

__ 2 3 __ 5 6 __ 8 __ 10

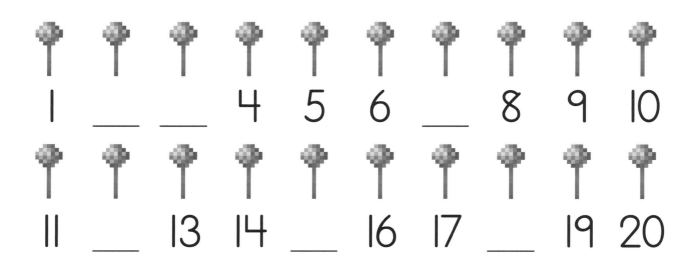

1 __ __ 4 5 6 __ 8 9 10

11 __ 13 14 __ 16 17 __ 19 20

MINECRAFT FACT: Relocate hives close to flowers so they can produce honey.

Write the numbers that come before or after each beehive.

13

_____  _____

18

_____ _____ 18

18

 _____ _____

14

_____ 14 _____

Copy the numbers from these bees into the spaces in order to create a number line.

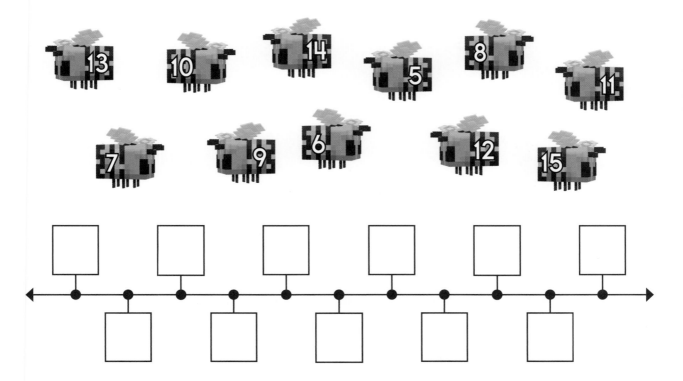

With the pollen they collect from flowers, the bees will pollinate your crops and help them grow.

Draw a **circle** (O) around the group that has the **most** flowers. Draw a **square** (□) around the group that has the **fewest** flowers.

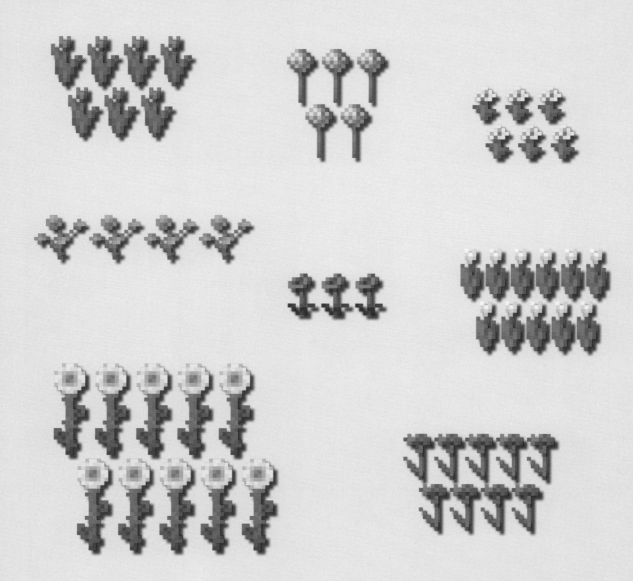

What did the sneaky bee say? "Hive got a secret!"

The bees are on their way! Help them reach the field of flowers by drawing a path from **START** to **END**. You can only pass through a number if it is bigger than the one before it.

START

3
5

3
6
4
2
1
6
5
6
2
9
8
7
1
7
8
9
3
2
12

8
12
3
19
7
8
10
18
10
14
17
11   13
15
16
15

17
20

END

You did it! Place your sticker here.

MINECRAFT MISSION

Minecraft bees are so helpful. Find more of them with this mission!

This mission sends you on a search *inside* this book. There are items hidden in the top borders of most pages!

Search the top borders for **bees** (🐝) to join the colony. But wait! You can only capture a bee if the number on it is **greater than 5** but **less than 15**.

Write those numbers in the spaces below.

Then find the correct sticker and place it in the lower corner to celebrate!

_____   _____   _____

_____   _____   _____

_____   _____

MINECRAFT
GATHER

MINECRAFT
CRAFT

SET UP SHOP

Make a workshop in your home. Then you can craft new tools and get to work!

In this adventure, you will....

Craft using workstations.

Mine fuel.

Smelt iron.

Create slabs and stairs.

Let's get started!

With different types of workstations, you can make new things.

Trace, then write big **Q**.

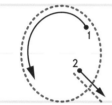

Trace, then write little **q**.

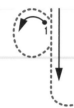

Draw a line from the blast furnace to all the ore with the letter **Q** or **q**.

MINECRAFT FACT: There are thirteen different workstations, each with a unique purpose.

Trace, then write big **R**.

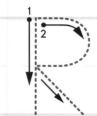

Trace, then write little **r**.

Circle every **R** and **r**.

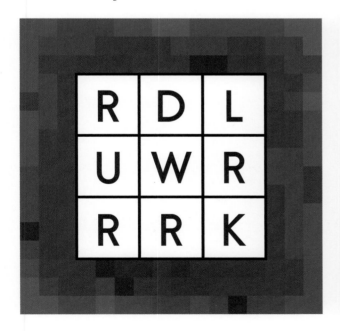

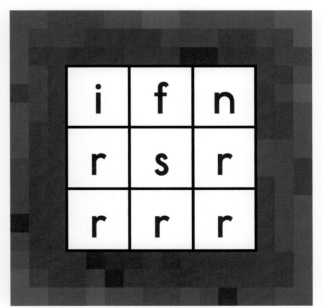

Mine coal to fill your blast furnace and smoker.

Trace, then write big **S**.

Trace, then write little **s**.

Trace, then write big **T**.

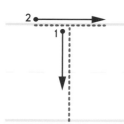

Trace, then write little **t**.

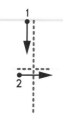

MINECRAFT FACT: Coal, wood, kelp, and lava can be used as fuel to smelt ores.

Find a path through the mine from **START** to **END**, and collect coal along the way. You can only touch coal with an **S**, **s**, **T**, or **t**.

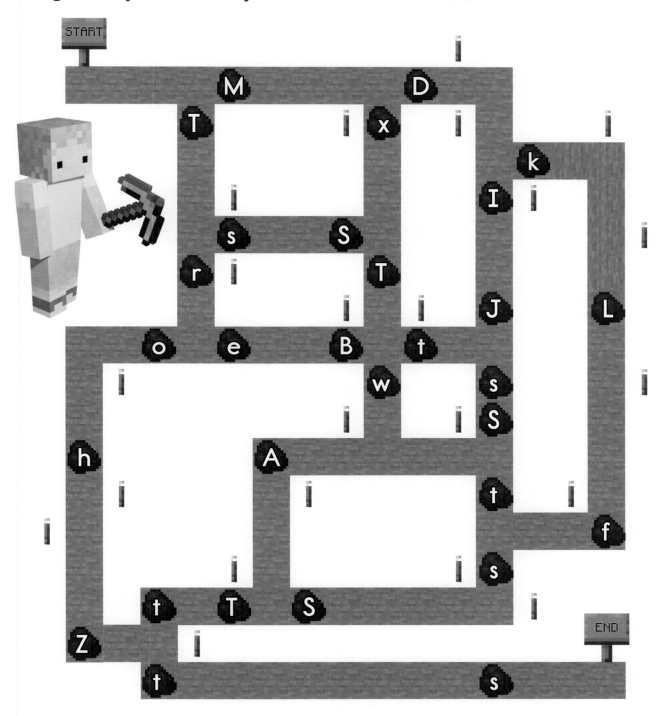

Smelt iron for weapons in your blast furnace.

Trace, then write big **U**.

Trace, then write little **u**.

Trace, then write big **V**.

Trace, then write little **v**.

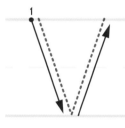

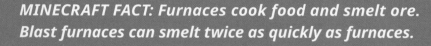

MINECRAFT FACT: Furnaces cook food and smelt ore.
Blast furnaces can smelt twice as quickly as furnaces.

Trace, then write big **W**.

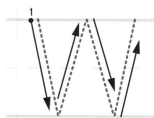

Trace, then write little **w**.

Draw **U** to connect all the **shovels** (⛏). Draw **V** to connect all the **axes** (🪓). Draw **W** to connect all the **swords** (🗡).

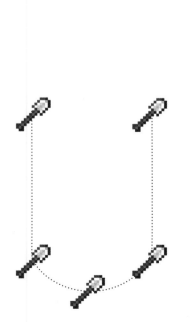

Use the stone cutter to make slabs and stairs for your workshop area.

Trace, then write big **X**.

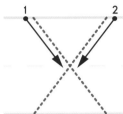

Trace, then write little **x**.

Trace, then write big **Y**.

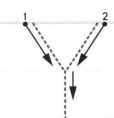

Trace, then write little **y**.

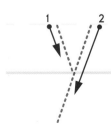

What did the blast furnace say when it got hot? *"I lava it!"*

Trace, then write big **Z**.

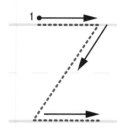

Trace, then write little **z**.

Circle every **X**, **x**, **Y**, **y**, **Z**, and **z**.

X			
C	X		
X	R	X	
D	X	L	T

x			
x	o		
p	x	k	
j	x	x	b

Y			
Y	Y		
Q	Y	A	
P	Y	O	L

t			
y	r		
y	y	y	
y	d	f	h

Z			
P	I		
Z	Z	Z	
F	N	Z	Z

z			
c	z		
z	m	z	
z	t	r	n

 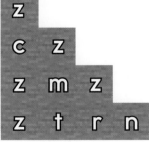

MINECRAFT MISSION

Your workshop is a great place to meet up with your friends.

This is a project *outside* of this book! Make a game to play with one or two friends or parents. Have an adult help you with setup.

You'll need:

- 28 index cards
- A pencil or crayon

How to set up:

- Write a word on each card.

Use these words:				
		queen	wolf	dig
dog	ice	plank	vine	block
cat	helmet	mob	under	axe
bees	gold	laugh	tool	yellow
armor	fish	king	stop	ore
nest	egg	jump	run	zombie

- Shuffle the cards and give five to each player.

How to play:

- Pick one card. Say the word and its first letter.

- If a player has a word that starts with the next letter in the alphabet, they have to give you that card. You keep going and call out a word from another card.

- If no one has the word that starts with the next letter, draw a new card. Then it's the next player's turn.

- The first person to have ten cards wins the game!

MINECRAFT CRAFT

Great job! You earned a badge! Place your sticker here.

TAME

WHAT FRIENDS ARE FOR

Minecraft can be a dangerous place. It helps to have a friend to explore with.

In this adventure, you will....

Search for a wolf.

Tame with bones.

Change a collar.

Feed your new friend.

Let's get started!

Find a wolf to become your companion.

Write the number of wolves under each group. Then **add** them together.

 +  =

_____

_____   _____

  +   =

_____

_____   _____

+   =

_____

_____   _____

MINECRAFT FACT: Wolves are most commonly found in packs of four, and they often spawn in forests and wooded hills.

Solve each of the **addition** problems on the paths below. Then circle the path where all the solutions equal **9**.

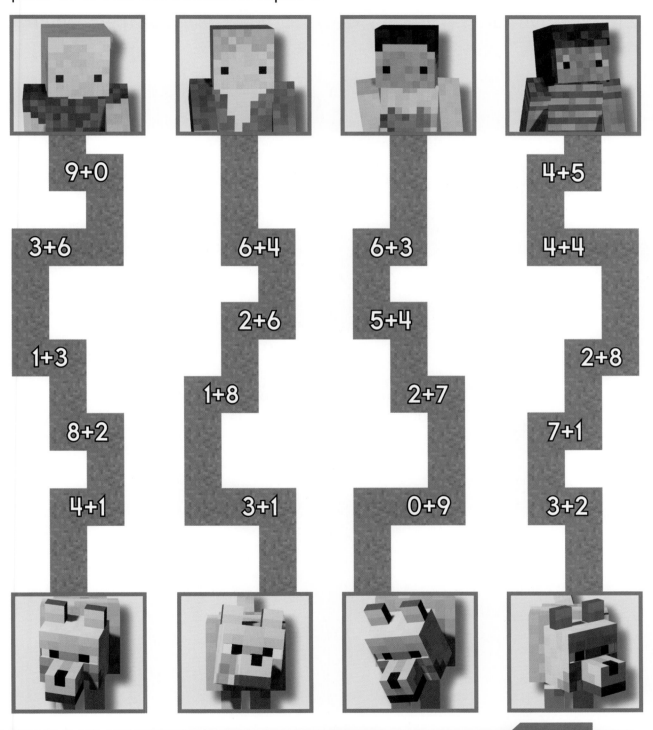

9+0

3+6

1+3

8+2

4+1

6+4

2+6

1+8

3+1

6+3

5+4

2+7

0+9

4+5

4+4

2+8

7+1

3+2

Wolves love bones! Get bones from skeletons to tame your wolf.

Write the number of skeletons under each group. Then **add** them together.

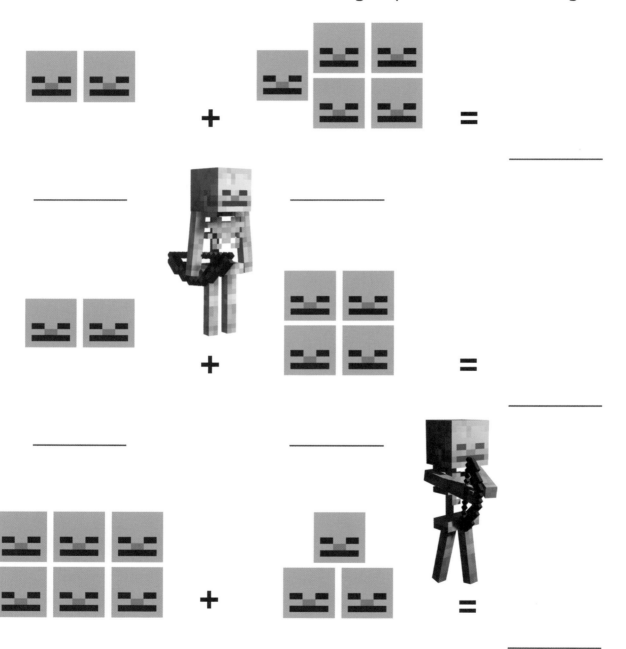

$+$ $=$

_____ _____

_____

$+$ $=$

_____

_____ _____

$+$ $=$

_____ _____

_____

Write the number of bones next to each box. **Add** them together and write the total under the line.

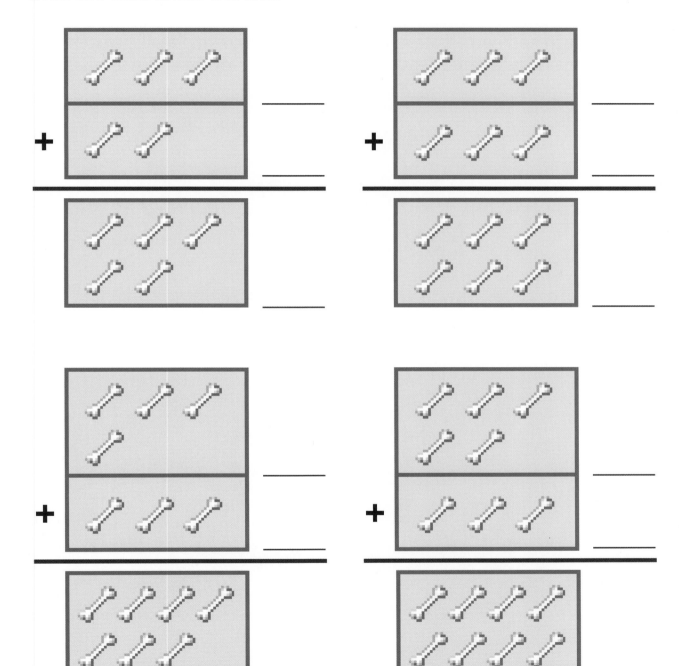

With dye, you can change the color of your wolf's collar.

Write how many tamed wolves there are in each group. Then write how many in each group have the correct color collar. Finally, write the amount that is left. The first one has been done for you.

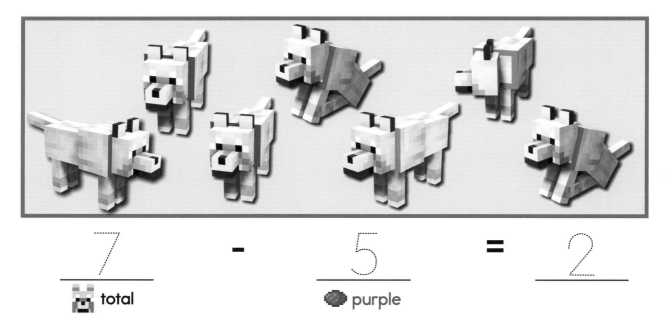

$$\underline{7} - \underline{5} = \underline{2}$$

total   purple

$$\underline{} - \underline{} = \underline{}$$

total   orange

MINECRAFT FACT: Collars on tamed wolves are naturally red, but you can dye them a variety of other colors.

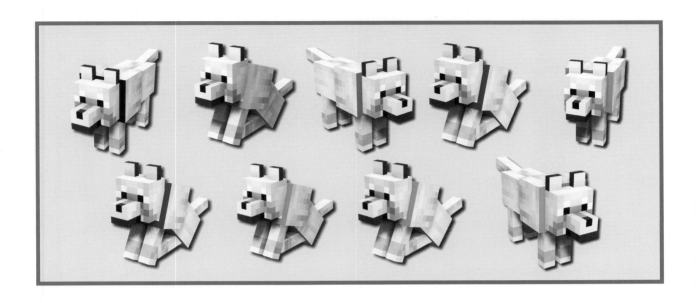

_____   **–**   _____   **=**   _____

total   blue

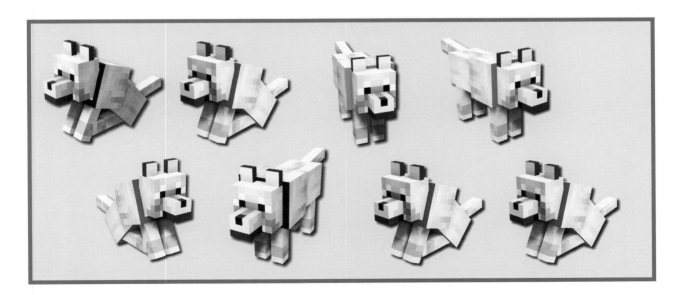

_____   **–**   _____   **=**   _____

total   red

You did it! Place your sticker here.

Feed some cooked beef to your new friend to keep it healthy and happy.

Count the **cooked beef** (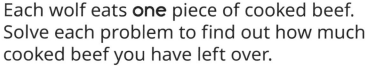) and write the number below each group.

Count the **tamed wolves** ( ) and write the number below each group.

Each wolf eats **one** piece of cooked beef. Solve each problem to find out how much cooked beef you have left over.

 -  = _____

_____   _____

 -  = _____

_____   _____

What do tamed wolves and trees have in common?   *Lots of bark!*

 - = _____

_____   _____

 - = _____

_____   _____

 -  = _____

_____   _____

There are many wolves to tame. Find them all in this mission.

This mission sends you on a search *inside* this book. There are items hidden in the top borders of most pages!

Search for pages with two **wolves** () hidden at the top. Write the numbers from the wolves into a row below, placing the larger number first. **Subtract** to solve each equation!

_____ - _____ = _____

_____ - _____ = _____

_____ - _____ = _____

Now **add** all three of your answers together... and give yourself that many cheers for completing this mission!

_____ + _____ + _____ = _____

MINECRAFT

TAME

Great job! You earned a badge! Place your sticker here.

EXPLORE THE OCEAN

You've reached the edge of an ocean. Head out into the open seas!

In this adventure, you will....

Get supplies and a map.

Build a boat.

Discover sea life.

Travel around an ocean.

Let's get started!

You're headed out to sea. Don't forget to bring food and a map on your journey!

The words **tag** and **map** have a **short a** sound. Write the letter **a** to finish each word.

c____n

g__p

p____n

t____p

s____d

r__t

b____n

n____p

Now say each word aloud.

MINECRAFT FACT: A Minecraft map will steadily fill in as you explore the world.

Circle all the items next to words that have a **short a** sound.

chicken

soup

bread

salmon

cake

melon

carrot

egg

beetroot

beef

rabbit

potato

cookie

apple

Now say each word aloud.

You did it! Place your sticker here.

Build a boat and load it with your supplies.

The words **ten** and **beg** have a **short e** sound. Write the letter **e** to finish each word.

f____d

t____n

p____n

g____t

Circle all the words that have a **short e** sound.

bed

wet

cat

boy

hug

sit

met

let

set

fan

Now say each word aloud.

MINECRAFT FACT: Boats are a quick way to travel. They are much faster than either swimming or walking.

Circle the boats that contain a word with a **short e** sound.

hen

den

box

gem

pet

bet

Now say each word aloud.

You've come across some new creatures in the water.

The words **big** and **fin** have a **short i** sound. Write the letter **i** to finish each word.

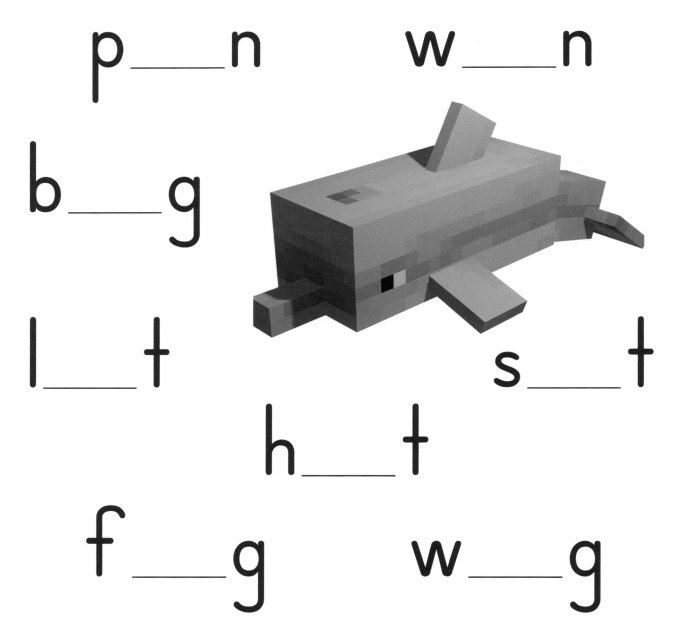

p___n   w___n

b___g

l___t   s___t

h___t

f___g   w___g

Now say each word aloud.

MINECRAFT FACT: Fish, dolphins, and squids are just a few things that live in Minecraft waters.

11

Circle the underwater creatures next to words that have a **short** i sound.

 kit

 box

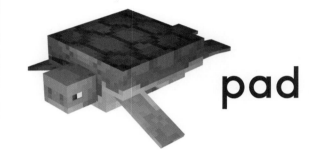 pad

 tin

 tip

 beg

 fog

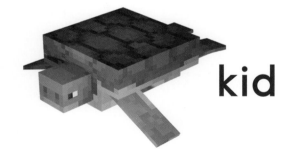 kid

 tag

 dip

Now say each word aloud.

You did it! Place your sticker here.

Use your boat to sail the seas, catch fish, and explore ocean islands.

The words **hot** and **pop** have a **short o** sound. Write the letter **o** to finish each word.

p___t   m___p

b___x   l___t

Circle all the words that have a **short o** sound.

big   hop   met

top   ran   sat

not   got   fin

Now say each word aloud.

Why did the captain put all his ships in a straight line?   *They were row boats!*

Find a path through the ocean from **START** to the island at the **END**. You can only pass through islands with words that have a **short o** sound.

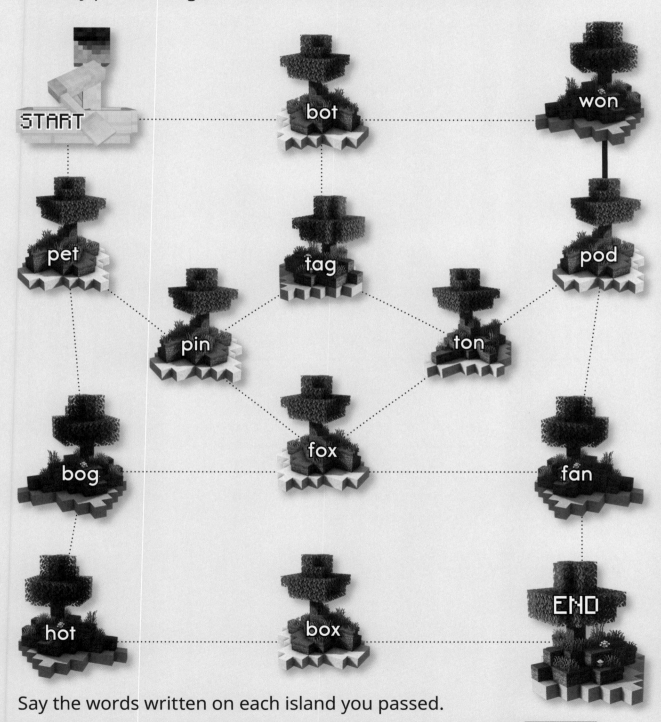

Say the words written on each island you passed.

MINECRAFT MISSION

It's time to play Minecraft *rhyme*-craft!

This is another mission that takes you *outside* of this book! Go on a quest to find things that **rhyme**.

Use your eyes—and your ears—to go on a rhyme search. Try it inside or outside your house.

Use the list of **eight** words below. Search for something in or around your house that rhymes with each word. Cross out each word on the list when you find a rhyme for it.

Use these words:			
rat	man	red	fin
zip	set	hot	tug

Once you find a rhyme for all **eight** words, celebrate by placing a sticker on this page!

MINECRAFT JOURNEY

Great job! You earned a badge! Place your sticker here.

BRRRRRR!

You've sailed into icy arctic waters. Chilly challenges are everywhere!

In this adventure, you will...

Avoid icebergs.

Find a shipwreck.

Travel over ice and snow.

Run from a polar bear.

Let's get started!

Hunks of ice float in the arctic waters. Watch out!

Color all the ice that is shaped like **squares** (□).

Color all the ice that is shaped like **triangles** (△).

How many chunks of ice did you color? _____

MINECRAFT FACT: Snowy plains are one of the few places you can find igloos.

Find a safe path through the ocean. You can only pass through spaces that contain **circles** (○).

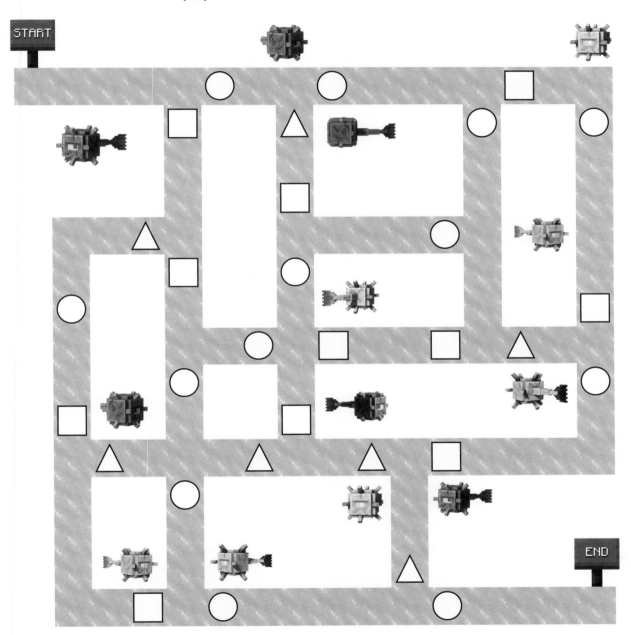

How many total **circles** (○) are on all the paths? _____

You did it! Place your sticker here.

You found a sunken shipwreck with a treasure of shapes inside!

Color all the **ovals** (⬭) red. Color all the **diamonds** (◇) blue.
Color all the **rectangles** (▭) green.

MINECRAFT FACT: Shipwrecks are great places to find treasure.

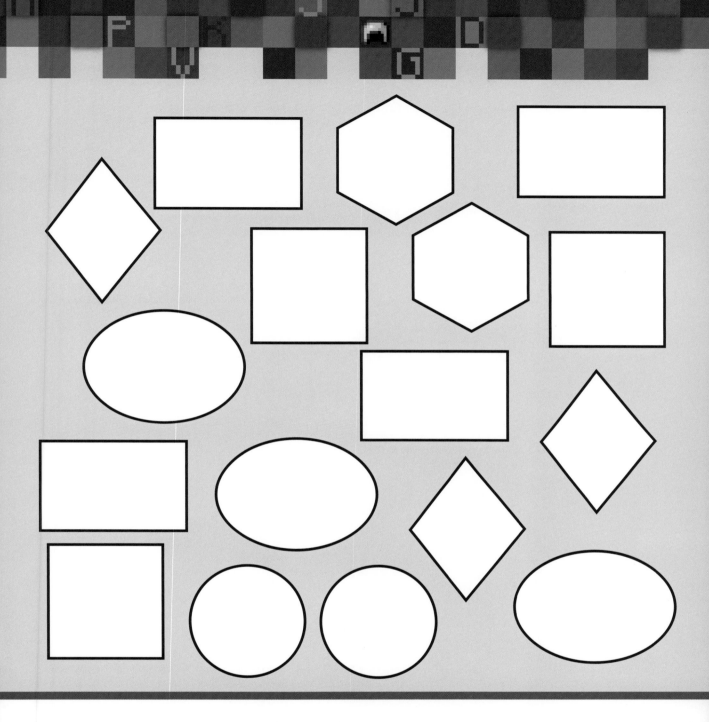

Count how many of each shape you colored. Then add them together.

_____ + _____ + _____ = _____

●   ◆   ▬   all

You made landfall on an arctic island! Build a snow golem to help defend you from any hostile mobs that may be lurking on the ice.

Add or **subtract** the numbers in each space. Then color them in, using this chart.

Use these rules:

3 = orange   4 = brown   5 = blue

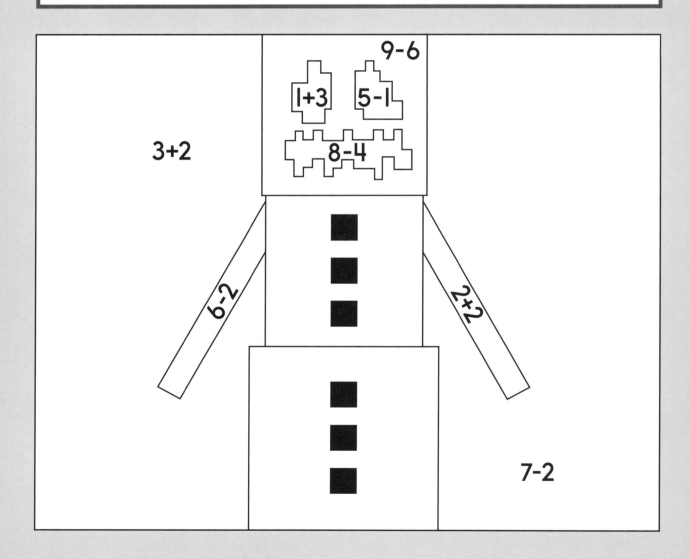

MINECRAFT FACT: *Sprinting and jumping on ice helps you move really fast.*

Begin at the blue **START** space and follow the rules below to reach **END**. Move up, down, left, or right in a single direction; to go back, reverse the direction you came. You can pass over **strays** (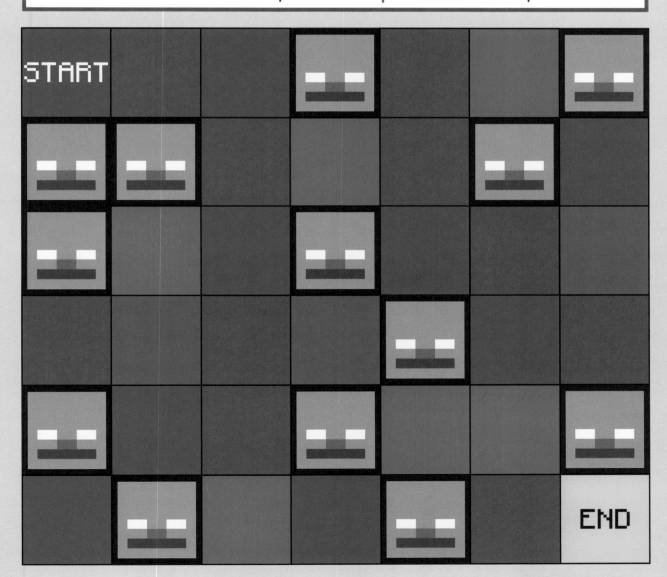), but you cannot end a turn on one! (Hint: There is more than one safe path.)

Use these rules:

Blue = Move **ahead 2** spaces   Red = Go **back 3** spaces
Green = Move **ahead 1** space   Purple = Go **back 1** space

You spot a polar bear. Don't get too close!

Pick the shape that finishes each row.

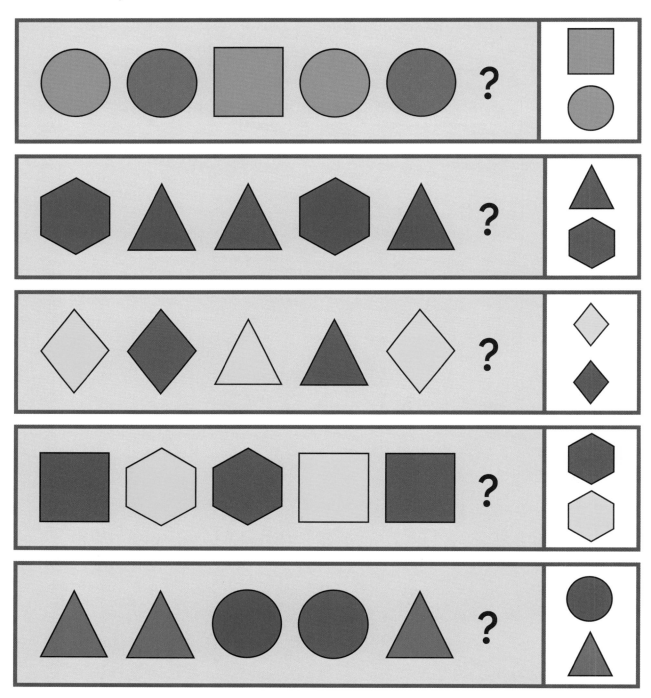

What did the polar bear do when it saw an adventurer? Pause!

Find a path from **START** to **END**. You can only travel along paths that follow this pattern: **circle, square, circle, triangle** (●■●▲).

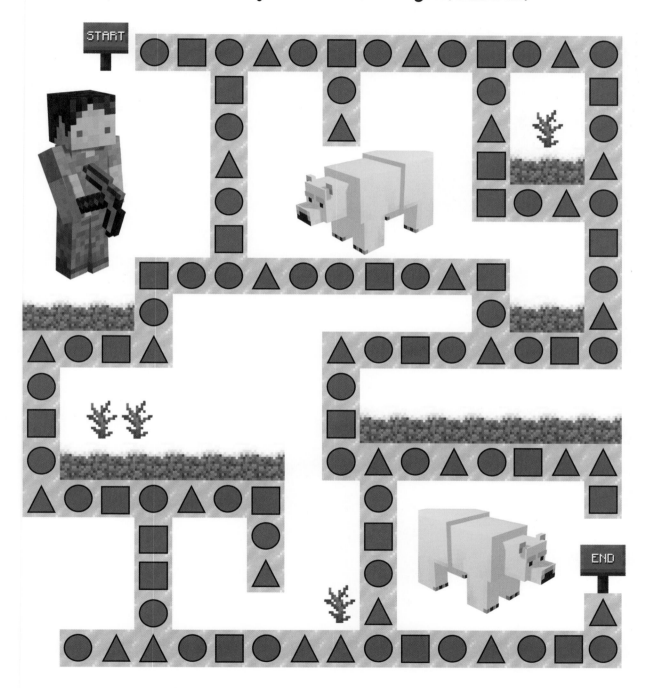

As you start your journey back home, make sure no more enemies sneak up on you.

Here is another mission where you must look for items *hidden in the top sections of this book*!

Search for **polar bears** (⬛). Each one has a number on it. Copy the numbers into these spaces.

_____ _____ _____ _____

Now write the correct number at the end of each row to complete the patterns.

1 2 3 1 2 ____

11 33 11 33 ____

9 8 7 6 9 8 ____

7 7 8 8 7 7 8 ____

Great job! You earned a badge! Place your sticker here.

DEFEND

ZOMBIE ALERT!

Zombies have followed you back to your village! This is your chance to be a hero.

In this adventure, you will...

Craft a sword.

Light up the night.

Protect villagers.

Battle zombies.

Let's get started!

Craft a sword to defend yourself!

The words **run** and **hug** have a **short u** sound. Write the letter **u** to finish each word.

b___g   p___p

t___b   c___t

f___n   r___n

s___n   m___g

Now say each word aloud.

Circle the **two** planks that have words with a **short u** sound.

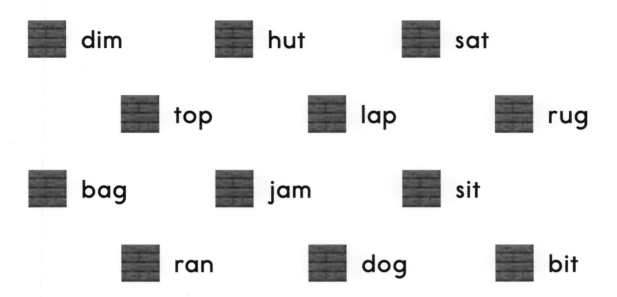

dim hut sat

top lap rug

bag jam sit

ran dog bit

Circle the **one** stick that has a word with a **short u** sound.

hat zap cat

ham fin big

pig yap car

dig hum bit

Light torches to make it easier to see...and to stop mobs from spawning!

The word **sky** has the vowel **y**. Add a **y** to finish each word.

sp____

fl____

tr____

sh____

Circle all the words that have a **y**.

top   bat   why

free   by   she

dry   can   cry

Now say all the words aloud.

MINECRAFT FACT: Creepers spawn in the dark, but unlike most hostile mobs, they do not burn in the sun.

Find a well-lit path from **START** to **END** so the villagers can avoid the zombies as they flee to safety. You can only go through words that have a **vowel** y.

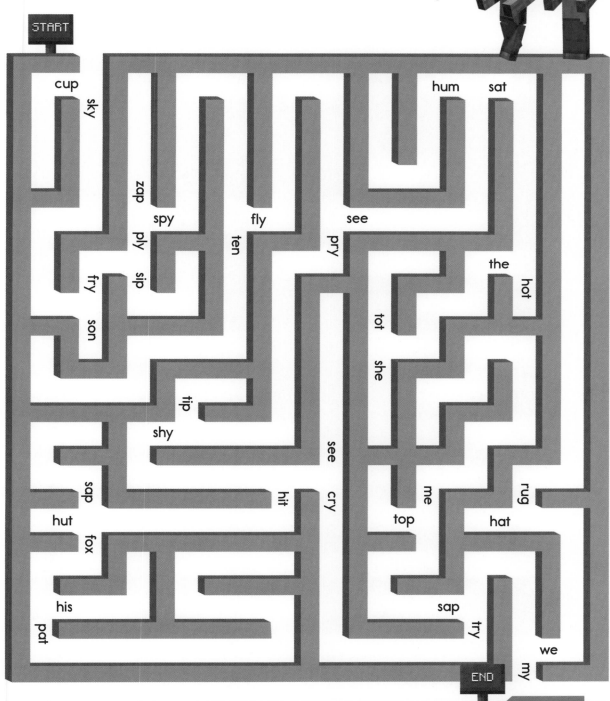

Ensure the villagers are all hiding safely in their homes.

The word **face** has a **soft c** sound. Add the letter **c** to complete each word spelled by the villagers.

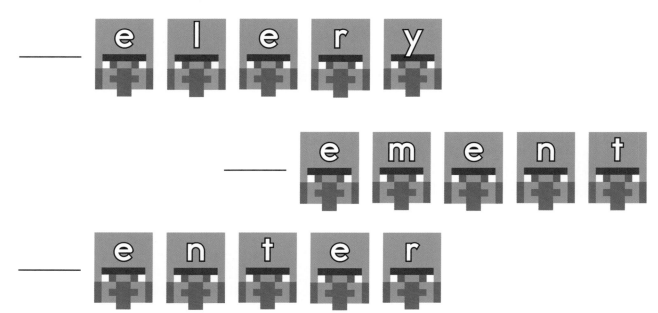

_____ e l e r y

_____ e m e n t

_____ e n t e r

The word **gem** has a **soft g** sound. Add the letter **g** to complete each word.

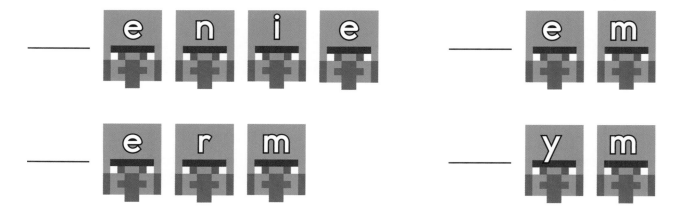

_____ e n i e   _____ e m

_____ e r m   _____ y m

Now say all the words aloud.

MINECRAFT FACT: Keep a village well-lit and it will prevent mobs from spawning nearby.

Circle the houses with words that have a **soft c** or a **soft g** to shut the doors.

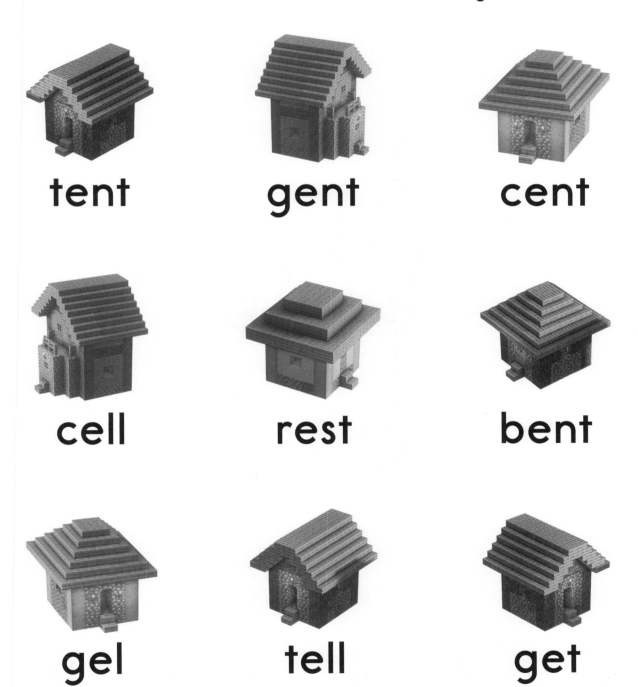

tent   gent   cent

cell   rest   bent

gel   tell   get

Now say the words you circled aloud.

The villagers are safe, but zombies are all around you. Battle them!

Trace each word that contains **sh** or **th**.

ship

this

toss

the

that

sun

sat

she

Cross out one zombie for each word you traced.

Circle all the words that have **sh** or **th**.

shot

stay · sheep

path · tot

son · she

the · shy

then · thin

shop · see

think

Now say the words you circled aloud.

You did it! Place your sticker here.

MINECRAFT MISSION

You saved the village. You're a hero in Minecraft... and beyond!

You've discovered so many things within these pages! Now try one last mission *outside* this book, and search for things in the real world that were part of your adventure.

Below is a list of **six** things to search for. Look in places like your kitchen or living room. You can search outside, too!

Check off the items as you find them. If you can find **three** of these things, you're an excellent explorer. If you can find all **six** things, you're a Minecraft Mission Superstar!

Super Scavenger Hunt:

• Something that is made out of wood

• Something that starts with a **soft c** sound (like **cent**)

• Something with all of the numbers 1–10 on it

• Something that is shaped like a **hexagon**

• Two different things that **rhyme**

MINECRAFT

DEFEND

ANSWERS

Pages 4–5

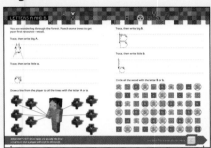

Page 7

Page 9

Pages 10–11

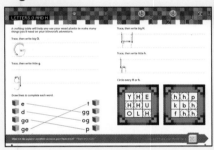

Pages 14–15

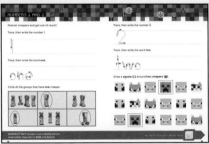

Pages 16–17

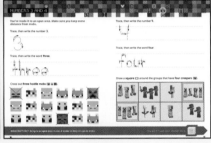

Page 19

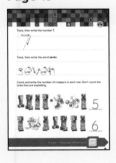

Page 21

Page 22

Pages 24–25

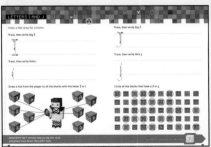

Page 27

Page 29

Pages 30–31

Page 32

Pages 34–35

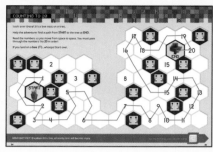

Page 36

Pages 38–39

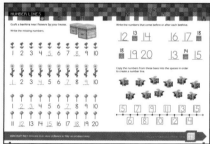

Pages 40–41

Page 42

Pages 44–45

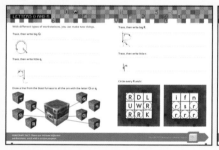

Page 47

Page 49

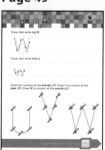

Page 51

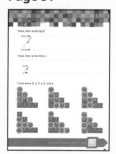

Pages 54–55

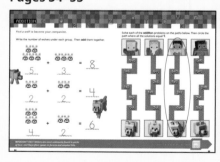

Pages 56–57

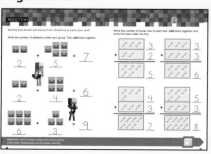

Pages 58–59

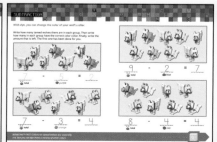

Pages 60–61

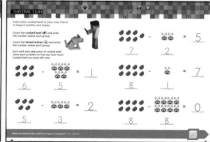

Page 62

Page 65

Page 67

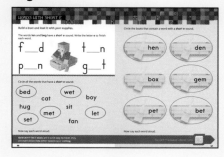

Page 69

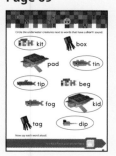

Page 71

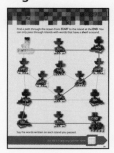

Pages 74–75

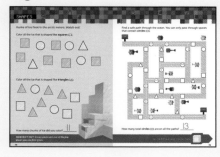

Pages 76–77

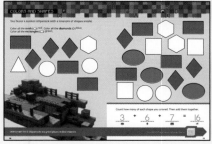

Page 78

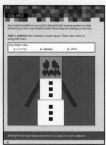

Pages 80–81

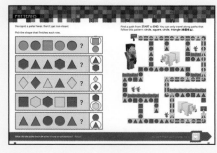

Page 82

Page 85

Pages 86–87

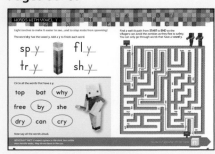

Pages 88–89

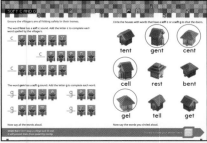

Pages 90–91

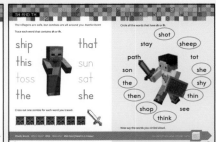

KINDERGARTEN
GREAT JOB!

MINECRAFT
ACHIEVEMENT

Let it be known throughout the Overworld:

YOUR NAME

has completed an adventure filled with MINECRAFT MISSIONS!